Additional Praise for Dani Johnson's Prospecting and Closing Script Book™

"WOW!!! That's about all I can say. The Script Book is SO EXCELLENT. Quadrupled my success rate with sponsoring. It's fun again."
~ *Greg Montijo*

"I have been a teacher, in the ministry, and most recently an attorney for 12 years – you would think that I would have had no problem talking to people about my new business. You would have been wrong! It took listening to Dani's CD's and working with her scripts to help me realize that all I need to do is talk and let "me" come through, no fear, no rejection, no wasted time. Since then, I have retired from the full-time practice of law and enrolled two attorneys and now have appointments to follow-up with two judges, some court reporters and clerks and a court bailiff! Oh, and the attorneys are now starting to ask me about this change in my attitude. I give credit for the change because I started reading and listening to Dani to on a daily basis. My focus is sharp, my confidence is up, my success is an answer to prayers."
~ *James Bauchert*

"Your Script Book and CD's have made cold calling a blast! It is a perfect tool for those getting started in this industry and a great refresher for those of us re-igniting the fire. It works great for me."
~ *Gary Klein*

"Thanks Dani, for your simple method!"
~ *Mike Crowe*

3

"Hi Dani. The Script Book is my business bible and now I recommend it to everyone. It's fantastic."
~ *Cornelia Doukas*

"We have had excellent results and have our new affiliates purchase the Script Book along with the initial training pack. It is actually a requirement in order to have our top leaders work with them one on one. I purchased 20 a few weeks ago for people to buy at our rally as we are introducing you into the new training. They were sold out within the first minute. Several of the people who bought them have enrolled in your live 2 day seminar!"
~ *Kimber Jarvis*

"Hi Dani!! First, I would like to say thank you. Your methods and teachings are totally changing the way I view my business and how I approach my prospects. We have searched for SO long to find a system that is easy to duplicate. Thankfully we were guided to you!!! I LOVE the Script Book and CD's and listen to them often."
~ *Debi Jones*

"The Script Book and CD's have made me much more comfortable talking with people on all levels."
~ *Vic Kalman*

"I think your Script Book is great. It is working very well."
~ *Maxine Elderd*

"Every time that I have deviated from your Script Book, my number of closes has fallen. So I go back to your Script Book, word for word!"
~ *Tom Sweeney*

"I love the Script Book. I have just about worn it out."
~ *Barbara Delville*

4

"I LOVE the Script Book! Thank you Dani for providing such a terrific resource. I have just completed your Prospecting and Closing seminar, which was fantastic! I am a new network marketer with a background in teaching and administration. Your approach is so easy to follow. Thank you!"
~ *Nancy Intermill*

"I have seen and used quite a few script books. If you use it (The Dani Johnson Script Book) verbatim, just like you say, it works great. I found it to be the best I've ever used!"
~ *Daniel C. Brawn*

"Dani's Script Book made it easier to prospect. The script language stopped the majority of the objections I was getting before I used her Script Book."
~*Valerie R. Clavivn*

"Let me just say that I could NOT have achieved the success I have so far without the use of the Script Book. It is the very first thing everyone in my sales force is told to get. Thank you again for all that you guys do at DaniJohnson.com!"
~ *Monica Tubbs*

"It's been a great help and resource for me."
~ *Bill Moccasin*

"I think the Script Book is great. It has given me the confidence to speak to prospective members/business partners. It's changing my thought process about what I'm capable of. I am sincerely grateful to my business associate for recommending you and your products."
~ *Trina Bickham*

"It (The Script Book) is excellent! I have it open in front of me at all times. Thanks for your help."
~ *Tim & Kat Sparks*

"The Script Book changed my business!! I had been working for about a year and was about to give in just because of people coming and going in my business. My confidence is now through the roof! My team is growing in leaps and bounds! I followed the scripts and my voice, comfort and confidence just came. It was fabulous! Now I DO the presentations, run my team meetings with many learning simultaneously and am about to hit the next level of leadership myself. Thank you Dani for sharing your talent and passion so we can learn from you and share ours too!!!!"
~ *Martha Smith*

"Hi Dani, thank you for the Script Book & CD's. I love them and think they are the most helpful instruments I've been given so far to develop my skills in my business."
~ *Diane Walter*

"I am new at using scripts and I love this little book of gold. It has given me the confidence to talk to leads and be successful in delivery of information they need to hear."
~ *Catherine Adams*

"In regards to the Script Book and CD's, I think the fact that I have built into my presentation the cost of acquiring this tool as a pre-requisite to getting registered in our business would explain my sentiments on it. To quote our thoughts on it and what one of my team members just emailed me. Dani Rocks!"
~ *Colleen Shea*

"I like the Script Book...it makes duplication simple!"
~ *Allison Vokac*

"The scripts are great! Keep up the good work!"
~ *Stephen Rockovits*

"I love using the Script Book. This book has bridged the gap between potential customers and me. Thanks!"
~ *James Briggs*

"Using a script from the Script Book, I recruited an individual who achieved promotions in the first 48 hours!"
~ *Nancy Horneman*

"Your Script Book is a GOLDEN TOOL!"
~ *Karen McDonald*

"I really like the Script Book and Training Audios. I have grown from the fear of picking up the phone and making calls. I am more comfortable prospecting and talking to people. The scripts are cool and it is working for me. May God keep blessing the work of your hands. I am looking forward to some personal coaching calls."
~ *Andread Mayers*

"The information in the Script Book is second to NONE!"
~ *Steve Drewett*

"We love the Script Book and it has helped our business tremendously!"
~ *Stephen & Trish Stewart*

"The Script Book is great and simple to read with the correct posture."
~ *Melva Calvin*

"I use Dani's scripts everyday and my business is growing because of it!"
~ *Yvonne George*

Dani Johnson's Prospecting and Closing
Script Book™

Dani Johnson's Prospecting and Closing Script Book™

ISBN: 0-9789551-0-2

Printed in the United States of America

TABLE OF CONTENTS

Introduction

Congratulations! You have in your hands right now the only Prospecting and Closing Script Book™ of its kind in the industry. These scripts were created by Dani Johnson and they will help you reach entirely new levels of success in your business. She has a long history of writing scripts with VERY high success ratios.

From her beginning days living out of her car, using quarters from a pay phone, she hand wrote a phone script that helped her close 24 out of 25 sales. That script was a critical element in her formula for success and was part of the "system" that she taught to others as she went from having $2.03 to her name to making her first million in 2 years.

The scripts in this book will increase your success ratios when speaking to new prospects. You will become much more comfortable "talking" to people... to the point where it becomes a fun and profitable game. Your confidence will soar, and so will your results. The scripts are very specialized but 100% "non-company specific". You can use them no matter what opportunity you are involved in now or in the future, and whether you are promoting a product or service.

Also enclosed as a bonus are 2 audio training CD's jam packed with live training from Dani herself as she gives you examples of each script so you can pick up the right attitude, body language, tonality and posture.

It is also highly recommended that you attend one of Dani's live 2 day seminars as this will give you a solid foundation that will increase success in every single area of your life while exposing you to the CORE^5 Profit Skills™ Dani teaches that are responsible for transforming businesses from failure to exponential growth. Attending a live event with Dani Johnson is an experience you will never forget as Dani's seminars have been the birthing ground for many 6 and 7 figure earners in the home business industry and beyond.

The Dani Johnson Prospecting and Closing Script Book™ & Bonus Audios you now hold in your hands have been the #1 industry success tool for eliminating rejection, increasing prospecting and closing ratios and duplicating organizational success in record time. Massive action equals massive results... so TAKE ACTION NOW! Use this tool immediately and daily. Get yourself plugged into other DaniJohnson.com resources and you will be on your way to experiencing the success you've been searching for!

We look forward to hearing your success story. Please write us at DaniJohnson.com/support and let us know how these scripts and CD's help your business grow!

May God bless and prosper you, your family and your business!

Hans T. Johnson
CEO, DaniJohnson.com

Some Helpful Tips

• The idea of these scripts is not for you to be doing the "selling". It is for you to be interviewing and sorting for the serious prospects.

• Use a process other than yourself to "present" the details of your company, opportunity or product. For example, use a web site, recorded call, live call, audio or video tape (CD or DVD), live meeting, or even a 3-way call with your sponsor/upline.

• Work as many leads and talk to as many prospects monthly as possible. It often takes up to 90 days to fill your "pipeline" and start really seeing big results. Once you build momentum, it will get easier and easier and your profits will multiply. Commit to a marketing plan and stick with it. If you are working leads, work them consistently!

• Practice the scripts on friends and family or other business associates. Many people have had success by simply asking a friend if they could "practice" a new script on them that they were learning. The friend ends up saying, "Hey that sounds interesting. Can I do it too?" Or... "Can I get more information about that?"

• Learn Dani Johnson's Core Rapport Methodology™ and the F.O.R.M. acronym to ask questions and instantly build trust with your prospects. You will discover their needs, strengths and goals during the Initial Contact phase with the scripts. Take notes and refer back to their needs, strengths and goals when closing and handling objections. F.O.R.M. stands for Family, Occupation, Recreation and Message. While it is very simple, it is a VERY powerful technique when used correctly along with other Dani Johnson Core Rapport Methodology™ principles.

14

• Use a follow-up system (personal call, thank you note, postcard, email autoresponder, etc.). Statistics show you will increase your ratios significantly by following up with good prospects.

• Keep your thinking on track by listening to Dani's training CD's regularly. Every successful person will tell you that reprogramming your mind daily with audios from other successful people is a big key to success.

• Realize that leaders continue to do the key activities that make them money (selling product and signing up new reps) even when they don't "feel" like it. So learn how to consistently make yourself do the things you do not want to do.

• Think long term. It may take some time to find your flow and get the results you desire. Set goals. Reinvest back into your business monthly – into your advertising and lead generation programs and most importantly into your education, training and motivation.

• Use the Appendix pages at the back of this book to help you develop your List of Resources, Company Story and Call Log Sheets. If you are looking for quality leads for your business, see our recommended vendors list available to all registered FREE members at DaniJohnson.com.

DaniJohnson.com
Prospecting Script

Script Tip!
SMILE WHILE YOU'RE ON THE PHONE. YOU ARE NOT A SALESPERSON, YOU ARE A BUSINESS DEVELOPER.

Script Tip!
F.O.R.M. your prospects. Don't assume you know everything about them. Ask questions.

Hi **"PROSPECT'S NAME"**, how's it going?
This is **"YOUR NAME"**, I'm calling you back.
You requested more information about working from home?
What can I do for you?

Do you have a pen and paper handy?
To save us both time, I need to ask you a few questions to figure out what information to direct you to.

Some Questions To Ask Are:

Are you currently working from home? *(if yes)* What is it? *(if no)* What do you do for a living? How long? What do you like about it? What do you dislike about it? Are you thinking of replacing your current income or just supplementing it? Are you married? Do you have kids?

Have you ever been self-employed or owned a home business before? Now, what level of income are you accustomed to?

16

What kind of income are you looking to generate in the next 12 months? Do you have some capital set aside to start your business?

You know **"PROSPECT'S NAME"**, our company has quite a standard for the people we are looking for. There's a lot of work on our part in setting someone up in a home business successfully. So we are looking for people who are absolutely serious about building a business and making money from home. So **"PROSPECT'S NAME"**, how serious are you about starting a home business? Tell me why?

Great, let me tell you about the company I work with.

> *Script Tip!*
> *Your company track record should be 30 - 60 seconds max. Stay away from* **PRODUCT/SERVICE** *information. See Appendix B on page 54 for a company track record outline.*

Now **"PROSPECT'S NAME"**, the person we're looking for has 3 main qualities; they are a team player, self-motivated, and dependable. Do you feel you have these qualities?

Great!
Do you still have a pen and paper handy?
Do you have internet access?
I want to confirm your email address.
What's the best email to contact you at?

FOR A WEB PRESENTATION

I'll be sending you a link to our website to make sure that you get the information. Hey by the way, do you have access to the internet while talking to me? Go ahead and go over to the computer now. I want to make sure that you don't have any problems downloading the information.

> **Script Tip!**
> *While they are getting to their computer, get them talking about what's important to them. Edify whatever presentation method you use, whether it's a website, live conference call, etc. Always edify your leadership.*

Were you able to download the information? Make sure and take really good notes because on this website is the information that you requested so that you can *(repeat their needs, strengths and goals)*.
(EDIFY THE WEBSITE)

FOR A LIVE CONFERENCE CALL

The next step is to direct you to a LIVE interactive call where you will get the information you requested so that you can *(repeat their needs, strengths and goals)*.

FOR A PRE-RECORDED CALL

The next step is to take you to a brief audio message about our company. This is where you can find the information you requested so that you can *(repeat their needs, strengths and goals)*.

FOR A LIVE MEETING or 1 ON 1 PRESENTATION

The next step is for us to meet in person so you can get the rest of the information available so that you will be able to *(repeat their needs, strengths and goals)*.

FOR A FAX MACHINE

Do you have access to a fax machine?
(If yes, fax them the information or give them your FOD# [fax on demand.] You can also get their mailing address to send them an information pack if you want)

Let me give you my phone number: **"YOUR NUMBER"**. We're pre-screening a lot of people right now. We'll be making a decision real soon, so the sooner you can go to *(website, live conference call, pre-recorded call, live meeting, live 1 on 1 presentation, fax machine)* the better. Depending on what your response is to this information will determine whether or not we'll work together and where you fit in on our team. If you're available on **"DATE & TIME"**, *(choose a day and time that's best for you)* I'll call you back and we'll see if it's a match and what your next step might be. So does **"DAY & TIME"** work for you? Ok, talk to you soon.

Script Tip!
Set an appointment and follow up with them. If on the web, it needs to be 15 minutes not 2 days. There is no urgency in 2 days. There is urgency in NOW!

Voice Mail Message Script

> **Script Tip!**
> *SMILE WHILE YOU'RE ON THE PHONE. YOU ARE NOT A SALESPERSON, YOU ARE A BUSINESS DEVELOPER.*

> **Script Tip!**
> *You are not talking to a machine, you are talking to a live person who will be listening to this message. Leave the message as though you are talking to a friend not a stranger.*

Hi **"PROSPECT'S NAME"**, this is **"YOUR NAME"**. I'm calling you back to get you the information you requested. We're doing some pre-screening interviews right now because it takes a lot of work on our part to establish someone in a home based business.

So if you're serious, give me a call back. I'll get that information to you and we'll see if you have the qualities of the kind of person we're looking for. At that point we'll decide whether or not we'll be able to work together and where you fit on the team.

My phone number is: **"YOUR NUMBER"**. Again, that's **"YOUR NUMBER"**. Have an awesome day and God bless!

Alternate Voice Mail Script *If* You Have A Compelling Story To Tell

---

> **Script Tip!**
> *SMILE WHILE YOU'RE ON THE PHONE. YOU ARE NOT A SALESPERSON, YOU ARE A BUSINESS DEVELOPER.*

> **Script Tip!**
> *You are not talking to a machine, you are talking to a live person who will be listening to this message. Leave the message as though you are talking to a friend not a stranger.*

Hi **"PROSPECT'S NAME"**, this is **"YOUR NAME"**, calling you back to get you the information you requested. I've been with our company for ___ months and we've made ___ working part time.

We're doing some pre screening interviews right now because it takes a lot of work on our part to establish someone in their own home based business.

So if you're serious, give me a call back. I'll get that information to you and we'll see if you have the qualities of the kind of person we're looking for. At that point we'll decide whether or not we'll be able to work together and where you fit on the team.

My phone number is: **"YOUR NUMBER"**. Again, that's **"YOUR NUMBER"**. Have an awesome day and God bless!

21

Follow-Up & Closing Script

> **Script Tip!**
> SMILE WHILE YOU'RE ON THE PHONE. YOU ARE NOT
> A SALESPERSON, YOU ARE A BUSINESS DEVELOPER.
>
> *When handling objections do not be on the defense.*
> *Remember, they are afraid of "risk". Just pile up the*
> *worth by repeating their needs, strengths and goals back*
> *to them.*

Hi **"PROSPECT'S NAME",** how's it going? *(build rap-port)* Did you get a chance to review that information yet? Great.

> **Script Tip!**
> *This is a good place to insert your personal*
> *testimony. For example: "Prior to getting started...*

1. What did you like about what you saw? *(heard, read, etc.)*

2. Tell me more about that. *(Let them sell themselves. Take notes here, you should already have some notes from your first phone call with them.)*

3. Okay, **"PROSPECT'S NAME",** do you want to make a little or a lot?

4. What for?

5. **"PROSPECT'S NAME",** at your current job, how long will it take you to be able to *(list the needs, strengths and goals they just gave you)?*

6. Where do you see yourself getting started, at the bottom working slowly towards *(repeat their needs, strengths and goals)* or do you want to be in a position where you can earn 2 times the amount of money for the same amount of work and effort?

Great! Welcome aboard. How do you want your name spelled on your checks?

DaniJohnson.com

Group Presentation With 3 or More

Script Tip!
SMILE WHILE YOU'RE ON THE PHONE. YOU ARE NOT A SALESPERSON, YOU ARE A BUSINESS DEVELOPER.

When handling objections do not be on the defense. Remember, they are afraid of "risk". Just pile up the worth by repeating their needs, strengths and goals back to them.

Hi **"PROSPECT'S NAME",** how's it going? *(build rapport)*

1. Okay, **"PROSPECT'S NAME",** do you want to make a little or a lot?

2. Where do you see yourself getting started, at the bottom working slowly towards *(repeat their needs, strengths and goals)* or do you want to be in a position where you can earn 2 times the amount of money for the same amount of work and effort?

Great! Welcome aboard. How do you want your name spelled on your checks?

Alternate Closing Script

> **Script Tip!**
> *SMILE WHILE YOU'RE ON THE PHONE. YOU ARE NOT A SALESPERSON, YOU ARE A BUSINESS DEVELOPER.*

The next step is to try our **"PRODUCT/SERVICE"** and let your body tell you whether or not it works. At that point you will know if this is something that you can really get behind.They have a risk-free trial. *(tell them about your guarantee)*

Most people start off with **"PRODUCT/SERVICE"** which is our most popular **"PRODUCT/SERVICE"** and it's only **"SPECIAL PRICE"**.

> **Script Tip!** *Share a few testimonials here.*

So if you'd like we can get the order department on the line right now and get your order placed so you can have that product in your hands as soon as possible. Then I'd suggest getting familiar with our support and marketing and training systems while you're waiting for your **"PRODUCT/SER-VICE"** to arrive. Hold the line and we will get that order taken care of for you. *(3-way your prospect into your order department or take down their order information)*

> **Script Tip!**
> *When handling objections do not be on the defense. Remember, they are afraid of "risk". Just pile up the worth by repeating their needs, strengths and goals back to them.*

Really... tell me more about that?
(Keep asking to get to the root issue)

You know **"PROSPECT'S NAME",** remember how you were saying that you want to *(repeat their needs, strengths and goals back to them, sell them on THEIR dreams and goals).*

So are you serious about that? How serious?

So are you willing to learn, work and try at something that maybe can give you a chance? Just give it a shot, this is a chance to get *(list some of their goals).*

Great, here's your next step. Let's get you on the phone with the order department and get your account setup. Let me get some information from you first. (*Get order details, etc.*)

"PROSPECT'S NAME", is it that you really don't have the **"PROSPECT'S OBJECTION"** *(money, time, etc.)* and you want to get started, or are you just telling me you don't have the **"PROSPECT'S OBJECTION"** *(money, time, etc.)* because you are not serious at all and you don't want to hurt my feelings?

Referral Scripts

> **Script Tip!**
> *SMILE WHILE YOU'RE ON THE PHONE. YOU ARE NOT A SALESPERSON, YOU ARE A BUSINESS DEVELOPER.*

1. *(The prospect says no to your opportunity, but you have built a great rapport with them)*

Okay great, I really enjoyed talking to you and I agree with you that this is not for you. Who do you know that would like to *(insert* **"PRODUCT/SERVICE"** *benefits like: save $ on phone bill, insurance, legal services, lose weight, feel better, etc)*?

2. *(If you are following up with a customer and they liked your "PRODUCT/SERVICE")*

I am so excited for you that you are *(repeat their success on the "PRODUCT/SERVICE")*. Who do you know who also wants to *(repeat their results again)*?

3. *(If you have a friend or business associate you've previously spoken to)*

Hey **"PROSPECT'S NAME"**, how are things going for you? *(**F.O.R.M.** your prospect)*

We are expanding our business and we need your help. Who do you know who would want to *(list some benefits like: to make extra money, pay off debt, pay kids college tuition, etc)*?

Warm Market Scripts

Test Market Approach #1

> **Script Tip!**
> *SMILE WHILE YOU'RE ON THE PHONE. YOU ARE NOT A SALESPERSON, YOU ARE A BUSINESS DEVELOPER.*

> **Script Tip!**
> *F.O.R.M. your warm contacts. Don't assume you know everything about them. CREATE URGENCY AND EXCITEMENT. Be yourself and be casual. No one likes pushy sales people. Schedule a time to talk with them so that they can get all the information. **Follow-up is the key to success.***

Hey **"PROSPECT'S NAME",** how's it going? *(F.O.R.M. your prospect)* I was wondering if you would be willing to help me out with something?

We have been looking for a way to *(get out of debt, pay off our car, stay home with kids, increase our income, etc).* After carefully searching for a solution we found something.

But before we completely get ourselves in too deep, we are first doing a test market through a few friends we trust will give us an honest assessment. It's kind of a "look under the hood and test drive before we buy" kind of thing.

So would you be willing to test something out for me? Great, when can we get together?

Test Market Approach #2

> **Script Tip!**
> *SMILE WHILE YOU'RE ON THE PHONE. YOU ARE NOT A SALESPERSON, YOU ARE A BUSINESS DEVELOPER.*

> **Script Tip!**
> *F.O.R.M. your warm contacts. Don't assume you know everything about them. CREATE URGENCY AND EXCITEMENT. Be yourself and be casual. No one likes pushy sales people. Schedule a time to talk with them so that they can get all the information. **Follow-up is the key to success.***

If you have a good business reputation use this script.

Hey **"PROSPECT'S NAME"**, how's it going? *(F.O.R.M. your prospect)* Hey, can I get your help with something?

I've got this new thing I'm doing a test market with. I'm thinking it might really take off because I am working with *(name of successful person you're working with)* and they have *(list some results they've created)*.

But before I commit fully to this advertising campaign, we are doing a test market with a few key people to get an honest assessment to see if it's something people would use monthly and refer to other people.

So would you be willing to test something out for me? I'd really value your feedback.

Great, when can we get together?

Practice Approach #1

Script Tip!
SMILE WHILE YOU'RE ON THE PHONE. YOU ARE NOT A SALESPERSON, YOU ARE A BUSINESS DEVELOPER.

Script Tip!
F.O.R.M. *your warm contacts. Don't assume you know everything about them.* CREATE URGENCY AND EXCITEMENT. *Be yourself and be casual. No one likes pushy sales people. Schedule a time to talk with them so that they can get all the information.* ***Follow-up is the key to success.***

Hey **"PROSPECT'S NAME"**, how's it going? *(F.O.R.M. your prospect)* I know you are really busy with all that you have going on in your life and I almost didn't call you because of your schedule. But, I really need your help.

We have been looking for a way to *(get out of debt, pay off our car, stay home with kids, increase our income, etc)* and I believe we found a way. But, before I begin my national advertising campaign I was hoping I would gain some experience by first practicing with you.

Do you think you could help me out?
Great, when can we get together?

(Schedule for a web presentation, conference call, 1 on 1 presentation, etc.)

Practice Approach #2

If you are working on a promotion, use this script.

Hey **"PROSPECT'S NAME"**, can I get your help with
something? *(F.O.R.M. your prospect)* I've been working
on moving up to the next promotion in my career *(or a new
career)*. In order for me to get promoted I have to work on
a few key skill sets.

So I need to practice on a few people and I was wondering
if I can practice on you? Great, when can we get together?

*(Schedule for a web presentation, conference call, 1 on 1
presentation, etc.)*

Practice Approach #3

If you are working on a bonus, use this script.

Hey **"PROSPECT'S NAME"**, how's it going? *(F.O.R.M. your prospect)* The company that I am working with has just put together a bonus structure and I am working really hard to catch that bonus right now and I was wondering if I can get your help with something? I basically need to get some practice so I can grab that bonus.

So would you be willing to let me practice on you? Great, when can we get together?

(Schedule for a web presentation, conference call, 1 on 1 presentation, etc.)

Practice Approach #4

> **Script Tip!**
> SMILE WHILE YOU'RE ON THE PHONE. YOU ARE NOT A SALESPERSON, YOU ARE A BUSINESS DEVELOPER.

> **Script Tip!**
> *F.O.R.M.* your warm contacts. Don't assume you know everything about them. *CREATE URGENCY AND EXCITEMENT.* Be yourself and be casual. No one likes pushy sales people. Schedule a time to talk with them so that they can get all the information. **Follow-up is the key to success.**

If you are a brand new person who just got started with the business, use this script.

Hey **"PROSPECT'S NAME"**, how's it going? *(F.O.R.M. your prospect)* Hey, listen I just made a career move and I am needing to get some practice and some experience and I am really wanting to impress the person who is training me.

So I was wondering if I can get some experience by practicing on you? Great, when can we get together?

(Schedule for a web presentation, conference call, 1 on 1 presentation, etc.)

Opinion Approach

Hey **"PROSPECT'S NAME"**, how's it going? *(F.O.R.M. your prospect)* I need your help with something. Can you look over this information and tell me what you think?

(Schedule for a web presentation, conference call, 1 on 1 presentation, etc.)

Networking/Professional Approach

> **Script Tip!**
> *SMILE WHILE YOU'RE ON THE PHONE. YOU ARE NOT A SALESPERSON, YOU ARE A BUSINESS DEVELOPER.*

> **Script Tip!**
> *F.O.R.M. your warm contacts. Don't assume you know everything about them. CREATE URGENCY AND EXCITEMENT. Be yourself and be casual. No one likes pushy sales people. Schedule a time to talk with them so that they can get all the information. **<u>Follow-up is the key to success.</u>***

Hey **"PROSPECT'S NAME"**, how's it going? *(F.O.R.M. your prospect)* I am putting a list of approved vendors together. I am looking for a mutually beneficial relationship with a few key business people that I feel really good about referring business to.

Through our company, I am in contact with quite a number of people everyday that could benefit from your services and with my recommendation may choose to use you instead of your competitor.

The way I am going about choosing my approved list of vendors is like this... I'll be with a group of entrepreneurs on **"DATE & TIME"**.

What I'd like you to do is come down, bring some business cards and make some new contacts with these entrepreneurs. There's going to be an orientation and you'll learn a little bit about what our company does.

34

After the orientation, let's sit down and talk and see how we might mutually benefit each other.

And who knows, once you see what our company does, you may see it as something that might be a perfect fit with your *(insurance, real-estate, etc.)* business. And if not, that's fine too, at least you'll be able to make some new contacts and pass out some business cards.

So are you available on **"DATE & TIME"**?

Direct Approach

Hey **"PROSPECT'S NAME",** how's it going? *(F.O.R.M.
your prospect)* Hey, I have a quick question for you.

Choose one:
1. How would you like to capitalize on your people skills,
   contacts, expertise, experience and knowledge?

2. If there was a way for you to *(pick one: double your
   income, get out of debt, retire early, diversify your
   income, pay for kids college tuition, stay home with
   your kids, travel more, etc.)* would you want to get more
   information?

3. Would you like to have more fun while earning money?

4. Can you see yourself doing what you are doing right
   now for the rest of your life?

Are you serious about that?
Great, we need to talk. I'm working part time doing something I'm really excited about.

I'm not sure if this would be for you or not, but I think you should get the information so you can *(repeat what they agreed to - i.e. get out of debt, etc.)*
When are you available?

(Schedule for a web presentation, conference call, 1 on 1 presentation, etc.)

Face to Face Conversation Approach

> **Script Tip!**
> SMILE WHILE YOU'RE ON THE PHONE. YOU ARE NOT A SALESPERSON, YOU ARE A BUSINESS DEVELOPER.

> **Script Tip!**
> **F.O.R.M.** your warm contacts. Don't assume you know everything about them. CREATE URGENCY AND EXCITEMENT. Be yourself and be casual. No one likes pushy sales people. Schedule a time to talk with them so that they can get all the information. **Follow-up is the key to success.**

Hey **"PROSPECT'S NAME"**, you know you mentioned *(repeat what their need was)*. I work with a company that is expanding all over the country right now. I don't know if you have the skills and qualities of the person that they're looking for and I'm sure you're totally satisfied with your current job, but let's exchange phone numbers. I can get you some information of what they have available and then we can go from there. If it's a match, great, if not, that's fine too. At least it's a chance for you to *(repeat their need)*.

So when is a good time to call you?

(Get their number, email address, etc. and the best time to reach them. FOLLOW-UP and direct them to your website, recorded call, schedule them for a live meeting, etc. When you follow-up, continue to build a rapport.)

Well that depends of course on the kind of qualities and
skills that you have, and at this point we really don't know
what that is. It's at least a chance for you to *(repeat their
need)*.
If it's a match, great, if not, that's fine too.

So when is a good time to call you?

*(Schedule for a web presentation, conference call, 1 on 1
presentation, etc.)*

Face to Face Conversation Approach Call Back

> **Script Tip!**
> *SMILE WHILE YOU'RE ON THE PHONE. YOU ARE NOT A SALESPERSON, YOU ARE A BUSINESS DEVELOPER.*

> **Script Tip!**
> *F.O.R.M.* *your warm contacts. Don't assume you know everything about them. CREATE URGENCY AND EXCITEMENT. Be yourself and be casual. No one likes pushy sales people. Schedule a time to talk with them so that they can get all the information.* ***Follow-up is the key to success.***

Hi **"PROSPECT'S NAME"**. This is **"YOUR NAME"**. You and I met **"YESTERDAY/TODAY"** at **"TIME"**. How did the rest of your day go?

When we spoke last I told you that I would get you some information so that you would be able to *(repeat their needs, strengths and goals)*. Do you have a pen and paper handy? Great.

To save us both time I need to ask you a few questions to figure out what information to direct you to?

Some Questions To Ask Are:
What do you do for a living? How long? What do you like about it? What do you dislike about it? What did you do before? What did you like about it? What did you dislike about it? Are you thinking of replacing your current income or just supplementing it?

40

Are you married? Do you have kids? Now, what level of income are you accustomed to? What kind of income are you looking to generate in the next 12 months?

You know **"PROSPECT'S NAME"**, our company has quite a standard for the people we are looking for. There's a lot of work on our part in establishing somebody with our company and getting them trained and off to a good start.

We are looking for people who are team players, self-motivated and dependable. Do you feel you have these qualities? Great, let me tell you about the company I work with.

> ### Script Tip!
> *Your company track record should be 30 - 60 seconds max. Stay away from* **PRODUCT/SERVICE** *information. See Appendix B on page 54 for a company track record outline.*

Do you still have a pen and paper handy?
Do you have internet access?
I want to confirm your email address.
What's the best email to contact you at?

FOR A WEB PRESENTATION

I'll be sending you a link to our website to make sure that you get the information. Hey by the way, do you have access to the internet while talking to me? Go ahead and go over to the computer now. I want to make sure that you don't have any problems downloading the information.

> ### Script Tip!
> *While they are getting to their computer, get them talking about what's important to them. Edify whatever presentation method you use, whether it's a website, live conference call, etc. Always edify your leadership.*

Were you able to download the information? Make sure and take really good notes because on this website is the information that you requested so that you can *(repeat their needs, strengths and goals)*.
(EDIFY THE WEBSITE)

FOR A LIVE CONFERENCE CALL

The next step is to direct you to a LIVE interactive call where you will get the information you requested so that you can *(repeat their needs, strengths and goals)*.

FOR A PRE-RECORDED CALL

The next step is to take you to a brief audio message about our company. This is where you can find the information you requested so that you can *(repeat their needs, strengths and goals)*.

FOR A LIVE MEETING or 1 ON 1 PRESENTATION

The next step is for us to meet in person so you can get the rest of the information available so that you will be able to *(repeat their needs, strengths and goals)*.

FOR A FAX MACHINE

Do you have access to a fax machine?
(If yes, fax them the information or give them your FOD# [fax on demand.] You can also get their mailing address to send them an information pack if you want)

Let me give you my phone number: **"YOUR NUMBER"**. We're pre-screening a lot of people right now. We'll be making a decision real soon, so the sooner you can go to *(website, live conference call, pre-recorded call, live meeting, live 1 on 1 presentation, fax machine)* the better. Depending on what your response is to this information will determine whether or not we'll work together and where you fit in on our team. If you're available on **"DATE & TIME"**, *(choose a day and time that's best for you)* I'll call you back and we'll see if it's a match and what your next step might be. So does **"DAY & TIME"** work for you? Ok, talk to you soon.

Script Tip!
Set an appointment and follow up with them. If on the web, it needs to be 15 minutes not 2 days. There is no urgency in 2 days. There is urgency in NOW!

** The following script is for EXAMPLE purposes ONLY! **

This is the script Dani wrote and used to go from living out of her car with $2.03 to her name and making $250,000 her first year! She then went on to earn her first million by the age of 23!

Product Retail Phone Script

> **Script Tip!**
> *SMILE WHILE YOU'RE ON THE PHONE. YOU ARE NOT A SALESPERSON, YOU ARE A BUSINESS DEVELOPER.*

Hi there. This is **"YOUR NAME"**. You called in reference to a weight loss program. Okay great! All I need to do is ask you a couple of simple questions to figure out which program to direct you to.

1. First of all, how much weight do you want to lose?

2. What type of diets have you tried in the past?

3. How do you feel these worked out for you?

4. We have been so busy with our promotion that we are having to do phone interviews to figure out who is really serious about losing weight, because there is a lot of work on our part to help you lose your weight. It's not just you going on another fad diet. This is guaranteed to work out for you. So we need clients that are absolutely serious about losing weight. So how serious are you about losing weight?

5. What is the main reason you have for wanting to lose your weight?

44

Okay great! Let me explain exactly how the _____ Weight Control Program works, because it's an extremely effective weight control program. Basically there are six items that are nutritional supplements that are targeted for specific areas of the body, like:

- To help with inches and cellulite
- To help block some of the fat & cholesterol out of the food that you eat
- To help keep your skin tight while you lose your weight
- To help you keep a good energy level throughout the day and help keep you from craving sweets – are you a sweet eater?
- It will give you all the nutrition you need
- And help to control and normalize your appetite so you don't feel hungry.

So, even if you tend to eat out of stress, depression, or boredom, or you might be a binge eater – instead of eating three cookies, you eat the whole bag – or you might be a nibbler who picks at food all day long, or if you're just a plain out-of-control eater, it will help to control and normalize your appetite so you just don't feel hungry! The average weight loss is up to 10 to 20 pounds per month ... and, what happened to me was... But I've got to tell you about a few of our clients (testimonial).

So the neat thing about the _____ Weight Control Program is that it supplies one of your meals a day, then you can eat whatever you want for your other two meals, like Chinese food, Mexican food, Italian food – it doesn't matter, because the program will naturally help you to cut back!

Right now we are running a special promotion. We will give you free counseling to make sure you are using it right and getting the results you want. That's all done by phone for your convenience.

45

The second thing is, we want you to take a "before" picture now, then an "after" picture of yourself, and then submit it to our monthly journal with a brief letter telling how much weight you've lost and how great you feel. So you and I need to work real hard together. It's a team effort, to make sure you lose your weight. If we use your story and pictures in our journal, you get $200 after publication.

The program is very inexpensive because it supplies one of your meals a day at only $1.75 a meal for one month's supply. Our nutritional supplement is incredible because you can put it into anything that you like the taste of, (i.e.: frozen yogurt, fruit juice, milk, hot chocolate, diet soda, lite ice cream – anything you want for one of your meals) Then eat whatever you want for your other two meals.

Then, the company gives you an all natural gourmet ____ that will completely control and normalize your appetite. You will not feel hungry. They are so delicious and totally satisfying! So you get one month's supply of all your herbs and vitamins, one meal a day, and all natural gourmet _____ to control your appetite for only $110 plus tax and shipping. Most of my clients like to take care of this with check or cash. Whichever is best for you is fine. Your program comes with chocolate, which tastes like Nestlé's Quick and Vanilla, which tastes like ice cream or cake mix.

When is a good time to get together so you can get on your way to being skinny, happy, and healthy? (Get good directions, and pick a time convenient for the client, or 3 way them into order department, or take order info yourself.)

Appendix A

Developing Your List Of Resources

Social scientists say the average adult has met 2000 people by the age of 21. One of the biggest success keys is to develop your list of resources to at least 200 people minimum.

Use this Memory Jogger to develop your list of resources! For your convenience we've enclosed a very good list. Another method that works very well is to use the yellow pages to jog your memory. Very simple, you just flip through each section of the yellow pages and as you come across each industry group you ask yourself the following 2 questions:

1. Who do I know who is a _____?
2. Who do I know who knows a _____?

Fill in the blank with the particular profession. For example, who do I know who is an automobile mechanic, auto body repair person, auto dealer, etc.

> **Script Tip!**
> *Do not prejudge people! The people you think will not be interested, will be. The people you think will be interested, won't be.*
>
> **You are looking for WHO THEY KNOW.**

Memory Jogger List:

Family
Mom and Dad
Sisters and Brothers
Children and Step Children
Nieces and Nephews
Aunts and Uncles
Cousins
In-Laws

Organizations
Church
Lodges
Schools/College
Community Groups
Health
Political

Athletic Contact
Fitness Center
Bowling Leagues
Concession Stands
Bicycling
Camping
Baseball Games
Tennis Matches
Hiking
Martial Arts
Weightlifting

Holiday Friends
Birthday List
Christmas List
Personal Phone List

Friends
Close friends & their friends
School/College buddies
Neighbors
Former neighbors
Workmates
Former workmates
Service buddies
Acquaintances
Web friends

School Contacts
Teachers
Principals
Associates
Coaches
School Aides
Secretary
PTA
Alumni
Parents of Children

Recreation

Restaurants
Nights Clubs
Bars
Parks
Beaches
Travel

Occupations & Education

Attorneys
Professor
School Teacher
Students
Principal
Counselor

Doing Business With

Co-Workers
Doctor
Nurse
Chiropractor
Service Station
Postal Delivery
Broker
Realtor
Accountant
Financial Planner
Bank
Mortgage Broker
Grocery Store Clerks
Insurance Agent

Homeowner
Landlord
Association
Veterinarian
Handyman
Travel Agent
Florist
Gardener
Manicurist
Hairstylist
Waiter/Waitress
Auto Repairman
Childcare
Dentist
Dry Cleaner
Housekeeper
Shoe Repairman
Clerks
Contractor
Roofer
Health Food Store Clerk
Health Club Associate
Masseuse
Pharmacist
Cab Driver

Entertainment/Artistic

Photographer
Interior Decorator
Artist
Graphic Designer

Choreographer
Musician
Director
Set Designer
Filmmaker
Video Producer
Web Designer
Actor

Government/City Employee
Fireman
Policeman
Armed Forces
Postal Carrier
DMV
Forest Ranger
Librarian
Elected Officials

Banking
Bank Teller
Loan Officer
Mortgage Officer
Financial Planner
Accountant/CPA
Stock Broker
Investment Banker
Escrow Officer
Title Insurance Agent
Bookkeeper

Church
Pastor & Wife
Members
Staff

Hotel/Restaurant
Waiter/Waitress
Busperson
Dishwasher
Cook
Chef
Front Desk Clerk
Driver
Concierge, Bellboy
Sales/Catering
Fast Food Employee
Housekeeper

Health
Nutritionist
Personal Trainer
Massage Therapist
Health Club Employees
Aerobics Instructor
Herbologist

Beauty
Hairdresser
Barber
Cosmetologist
Manicurist

51

Sales
Real Estate
Insurance
Retail

Transportation
Airline Pilot
Flight Attendant
Cab Driver
Bus Driver
Travel Agent
Mechanic
Baggage Handler
Ticket Counter Sales
Truck Driver

Business Professional
Entrepreneur
Business Owner
Executives
Office Managers
Trainers
Attorney
Psychiatrist
Psychologist
Personnel Director

Technical
Programmer
Systems Analyst
Data Entry
Computer Operator
Technical Writer
Engineer
MIS Manager

Construction/Property
General Contractor
Landscaper
Land Developer
Property Manager
Landlord
Electrician

Medical/Dental
Doctor
Chiropractor
Optician
Nurse
Dentist/Hygienist
Orthodontist
Physical Therapist
X-Ray Technician
Veterinarian
Paramedic
Ambulance Driver
Administrator

Miscellaneous
Secretary
Receptionist
Janitor
Garbage Collector
Housewife
Nanny
Babysitter
Housekeeper
Factory Worker
Plumber

Appendix B

Company Track Record Outline

This is an easy tool to use. All that is needed is for you to answer the following questions and follow the example on page 55.

1. State the age of the company.
2. Give your company sales volume.
3. State the number of representatives you have nationally and/or internationally. *(We have tens of thousands of representatives nationwide/internationally)*
4. Tell of the number of countries the company is operating in. *(We are currently doing business in _____ countries)*
5. Name 2 or 3 of these countries. *(Just to name a few we are in - give 3-4)*
6. State the number of clients you have nationally and/or internationally. *(We have tens of thousands satisfied clients all over the nation/world and because of their satisfaction they actually refer business to us on a monthly basis)*
7. Tell if your company is debt free and profitable.
8. Tell if your company is publicly traded.
9. Has your company been featured in publications and/or media venues? *(i.e. magazines, TV, radio)* If so, ask the prospect if they have heard of these media sources, then explain which ones you have been listed in and how many times.
10. Tell who founded the company.
11. State the name of your company. *(The name of our company is_____)* Ask the prospect if they have ever heard of your company. *(Have you ever heard of us?)*

54

Company Track Record EXAMPLE

> **Script Tip!**
> *Don't mention anything about the product or the FDA or patents on the "PRODUCT/SERVICE" when giving bullet points about your company. It provokes questions and you will lose control of the conversation.*

We are a 5 yr. old, $500,000,000 corporation. We have tens of thousands of representatives internationally. We are currently doing business in 14 different countries. Just to name a few we are in Australia, Japan and the United States.

We have tens of thousands satisfied clients all over the world and because of their satisfaction they actually refer business to us on a monthly basis. We are currently debt free, and publicly traded. We've been in a number of different publications.

"PROSPECT'S NAME", have you heard of Success Magazine? Entrepreneur Magazine? How about Forbes?

We actually have been in those publications 14 times in the last 2 yrs. We were founded by **"JOHN SMITH"** and the name of our company is **"XYZ COMPANY."**

Have you ever heard of us?
(if they say yes or no)
Great!

Appendix C

DaniJohnson.com Contact Sheet

Name	Phone	Email	Comments

	Appt	Follow Up	Comments

Appendix D

More DaniJohnson.com Resources To Help You Succeed!

If you've benefited from this Prospecting and Closing Script Book™ and accompanying training audios, then you'll find the following resources will help you even more.

Become a FREE www.WorkAtHomeProfitZone.com member – Access over 30 hours of training calls recorded live with Dani Johnson 100% FREE for you and your team. Register now!

FREE weekly training calls for you and your group with Dani Johnson every Monday night @ 7pm PST (10pm EST) Call 512-225-9400, pin 953953#.

Prospect & Close Your Way To Millions Home Study Course!
Who Else Wants to Learn How to Bring Tough Prospects to Their Knees as You Effortlessly Handle Their Objections and Watch Them Talk Themselves Right Into Joining Your Program? Get the Live DVD's and audios from one of Dani's Prospect & Close Your Way To Millions training seminars! Visit: DaniJohnson.com/product

Dani Johnson Live - Foundational Tools Essential To 6-Figure Success In Your Home Business on CD!
FINALLY... Training CD's Guaranteed To Turn You Into An MLM, Network Marketing or Home Business Pro! Get the audios from one of Dani's entire Live 2 Day Seminar on 10 CD's! Visit: DaniJohnson.com/product

1 on 1 Coaching!

If you would like to receive personal 1 on 1 training and coaching from Dani to help you master prospecting and closing using these scripts or coach you on ANY other aspect of building your business successfully, contact us at DaniJohnson.com/support or call 866-760-8255 for rates and more information.

Training Calls for your team or company!

To have Dani do a special Training Call for your team or company, contact us at DaniJohnson.com/support or call 866-760-8255 for rates and more information.

Attend a Live 2 Day Seminar with Dani!

Discover what's been holding YOU back and learn the EXACT tools that took this young woman from living out of her car... to making her FIRST MILLION in under 2 years! Visit: DaniJohnson.com/seminar for more information and to register for the next live seminar!

Attend a Live 3 Day Advanced Seminar!

Do you want to be equipped to develop a powerful sales force filled with top producing independent leaders? Once you attend a Live 2 Day Seminar with Dani then you will qualify for the Live 3 Day Advanced Seminar, Creating A Dynasty. For the elite who have attended both Live Seminars you may be chosen, upon meeting qualifications, for the DaniJohnson.com Mentoring Program. Visit: DaniJohnson.com/seminar for more information and to register for the next live seminar!

We want to hear from you! Please send your comments or testimonials to DaniJohnson.com/support. Thanks and God bless!

Notes:

Notes:

Notes:

Notes:

Notes:

Notes:

Notes:

Notes:

Notes:

Notes:

Notes:

Notes:

Notes:

Notes:

Notes: